My Life In My True Poems

True poems about love, relationship, my kids, my x-wife,
and hard times of spending in & out of jail and prison.

Jeremy Swanson

authorHOUSE®

AuthorHouse™
1663 Liberty Drive
Bloomington, IN 47403
www.authorhouse.com
Phone: 1-800-839-8640

Published by AuthorHouse 12/14/2011

ISBN: 978-1-4670-9431-3 (e)
ISBN: 978-1-4670-9440-5 (sc)

Library of Congress Control Number: 2011961105

Any people depicted in stock imagery provided by Thinkstock are models, and such images are being used for illustrative purposes only.
Certain stock imagery © Thinkstock.

This book is printed on acid-free paper.

Because of the dynamic nature of the Internet, any web addresses or links contained in this book may have changed since publication and may no longer be valid. The views expressed in this work are solely those of the author and do not necessarily reflect the views of the publisher, and the publisher hereby disclaims any responsibility for them.

A lot of people seeing me doing my poems and ask me if I will write them one. I wrote the book to show you my poems they are real poems about relationship, love, my kids, saying goodbye and few funning once too. I found I can write poems because when I was in jail, prison for a about 20 times, it start in 1985 to 2007. I felt a lot of feeling, I was guilt, mad, lonely, I hurt my kids because I was in jail & prison, I got divorce after 12 years, lost people in the life, I lost my jobs, a lot of money and ect. So I wrote this poems to let my feelings out, and learn but I didn't quit drinking so I lost every things it my life. I saved all my poems now. I read my poems a lot, I cry because I lost the trust of people, and hurt people because I wouldn't stop drinking it was my life. I thank god I am still alive I quit drinking 2 years ago. People like me again, and I like myself! I didn't have a Law to tell me I have to quit drinking, I make the choice by myself because I was bad, I couldn't talk, read, ect. Now I am getting good, so I what to see another people to learn and see about relationship, love, trust, and hopefully they will keep they ladies and men a lot time!

-*Jeremy Swanson*

Foreword

The reason I did the book is to share some of the trouble times in my life in hope that my kids and others will find a better way of life so they don't get trapped in one that can lead to death or imprisonment.

These poems you will find in this book are poems I wrote during all the time I was in jail and prison. It is about all the guilt and shame I faced and for putting my kids into a world of violence they had to grow up in, leaving they with broken promises time and time. The loss of a marriage and love and the constant thoughts of giving up on life and the feelings of a wasted life always being incarcerated.

I am still struggling with my life today and I write this as I once again sit in my cell. But there is always a new life out there patiently waiting all you have to do is want it.

I have four wonderful children that I need to say thank you to, because if it weren't for their love to keep me strong I wouldn't be here. Austin, Ashton, John, Jessica and to Sheila who stayed by my side all those 11 years. I wrote that in 2002.

2010 Today I'm sober, and have a beautiful life. I thank God that I'm still alive.

Contents

"Living in a child's world"

A child awake in the morning with a dream in his heart that the day be filled with laughter and love. For he gave his prayers to the man they say lives in the Heavens above. He hadn't asked for much just a hug and a kiss would let him know they cared. He just needed a little of that love he sometimes seen his parents had shared. But as much as he had prayed he knew the happiness never seemed to last. For he remember those times he stood watching, his eyes wide with fear again reliving the past. He loved them both so much, but it broke his heart to see them fight. So when the day was over he crawled into his bed and started the prayers again that night. He doesn't know why God doesn't answer, but again his little hands fold together praying for more. But sleep doesn't come easy for he continues to listen to the violence outside his door. Laying there he remember his dad once talked of a poem he wrote about a star that brought a tear to his eye. So he sat at the window searching for that one lonely star and found it buried deep in the sky. Then he wished upon that star knowing his dad had done the same.

And sadly
cause I know
he awoke he
love you" and
too," and that
throughout
laughing
But it
guy like
in his
at a face

he said, "I will make them proud somehow that I'm to blame." When went to his mom & dad and said, "I waited for them to say. "I love you was all he needed to carry with him his day. When he went outside he & playing and seemed to be okay. is a shame that a precious little him must carry so much sadness heart everyday. When you look of innocence look beyond more than just what you can see. Because a heart in a child is sometime in a world where it shouldn't have to be.

- Jeremy Swanson

I have my son John Grotberg draw is imagine.

Ashton

Austin

Jessica & John

"The master painter"

As he started the day he knew he had the biggest challenge he had ever faced. So he chose the purist colors with no time to waste. Each part he touched so lovingly and made the colors come alive and beautifully bright. And the work on this rare and lovely scene took him well onto the night. When morning came a smile came upon his face for he knew he was finally through. And it was on that day God has blessed me for it was then he painted you.

-*Jeremy Swanson*

"The little voice that saved me"

I dreamt one night that I tried to leave this world to rid myself of guilt and shame. Because I feared my life was just a drunken game.

AS I stepped to the edge a tear rolled down my face. Oh how bad I wanted to leave the hurt and loneliness behind and escape this place.

But suddenly I heard a sad voice come from within. A voice I've heard before and it said "Daddy please don't leave us again".

For there I stood thinking only of myself and not of who I'd leave behind. Were things really that bad or was I losing my mind.

So I stepped from he edge though still not wanting to face the day, but I'd try. For it was better that looking down from Heaven and seeing my little one cry.

-Jeremy Swanson

"When gold turns to silver"

I lay here every night thinking how the time with my kids was more precious than gold. No one knew that the day would come and our lives would again unfold.

We fished and we played and we always talked about things that came straight from the heart. We all had thought that this time spent together would be that new start.

Now tears fill my eyes when I think soon my kids little hands will be to big to hold. And missing the early memories of watching them at Christmas makes the warmth in my heart turn cold.

When you take away my freedom it effects a lot more than just me. It locks innocent little kids in a painful, lonely world where they shouldn't have to be.

Please forgive me for missing the fourth Christmas in a row and leaving you with broken hearts again. But I'll leave this place for the last time and change this hell we've all been in.

And make up for all the time that was lost and make more memories to hold. And make the change back in our live from silver to gold.

- Jeremy Swanson

"When will tomorrow come"

It's breaks my heart sitting behind these bars as my children continue to grow. How it feels to be ripped away from my life no one will ever know.

Their little hearts and mine will feel the lonely pain it brings. As the pendulum of time in life slowly makes it's swings.

No more holding hands, no more laughs, no more of that special time. Nothing brought more love and happiness in my life than knowing they were mine.

I have about twenty-four months in prison, my kids will be grown and life will have passed. I prayed for the day to see them again, but in a world like this time doesn't go fast.

I don't think about tomorrow because it seems like tomorrow will never come. But I think of them everyday as I watch the rise and fall of the sun.

2000 in prison To my kids, love and miss you,

-Jeremy Swanson

"The Wildlife"

Swan's health finally made him realize that he was watching his own life disappear, and he said "this is not who I am". All the Duck could do is look down from above, and she thought the Swan with his broken wings will never fly again. But he had the will and courage to make it back into the sky where he knew his life had been before. Because he took the time to rest and heal them broken wings making sure it never happens anymore. Other birds can not heal themselves and eventually give up on recovery. He didn't want to see himself that way he loved that Duck and didn't want to be just a memory. Duck loves it in the sky, if you have a broken wing you're not going to be by her side. But if you stand tall like the Swan you'll be by her side proud with your wings wide. So take a moment to see when one is trying give him or her a chance to heal. Don't walk away the pain is hard enough, more pain he or her doesn't need to feel.

If you have problems about drinking or drugs, you can fix that problem and you will be proud and fly away to a better world!

February 7th 2006 St. Louis Co. jail - Teresa (Duck)stad
- Jeremy (Swan)son

"Take me back"

So you think you made a mistake and found Mr. wrong. Well baby believe in me just read my poem and follow along. I remember when I first looked at those beautiful brown eyes, and that gorgeous long red black hair I was really in love for the first time. It didn't take long, your taste as our lips embraced was finer then any wine anyone can fine. You were incredibly beautiful and after the kiss the warmth of your smile made my heart melt. You have the most elegantly shaped soft and silky skin I have ever felt. Your pictures have so much beauty it brings me right down to my knees every time I'm in my cell. I show your pictures and people ask who you are, I say Teresa (Duck) the rest of your name I'll never tell. He is the maker of beauty and God made you as beautiful as any Angel could ever be. I lay here every night and wonder will I ever see Teresa again when I'm free.

To a special person:
Teresa Duckstad (Duck)
- *Jeremy Swanson "Swany"*

"The love of Duck and the Swan"

Nothing or no one, not even time and distance can take that away or tear it apart. I hope you remember that I will always love and miss you and keep you close to my heart.

I know life has been hard sometimes, but this kind of love is powerfully true. If our hearts remain together our love will always reign through.

My first hug, my first kiss and the first woman that I'll ever miss. How much I love her the world will never know the significance of this.

(I hope you think of me tonight when you close your eyes, I'll think of you.)

To: Teresa Duckstad
- Jeremy Swanson

"I hope I don't have to say goodbye"

You've saved me in a time of need while I sit alone in a cold concrete world. There are no windows to see outside, just pictures and letters form that beautiful girl.

So I sit behind bars suffering, not knowing when I will see the real world, but I know to this there is an end. But my deepest regret is if she leaves me behind, thinking I can't change and I'll fail again.

To have been together this long being miles apart, must have been fate. So I hope with a rose that my beautiful girl believes in me and will wait.

If she thinks of today as a new day and leaves yesterday in the past. I'll never make that mistake twice, I'll make them good times forever last.

So please Teresa don't give up because you and I know of relationships to hold on to, you and I are the one. I want to spend my whole life with you until all my days are done.

Teresa Duckstad

- Jeremy Swanson
(I wrote is poem in 2006)

"An Angel feather"

I dream of walking with you under the velvet sky and hearing the oceans waves wash upon the soft sandy beach. I think then as I look across the horizon that tonight our wildest dreams may be within reach.

For there is an undying love inside that needs what tonight can offer. And if we share together the desire to let our hearts free the loneliness in our heart will no longer suffer.

I have longer to hold you and to feel the heat of your body as it enfolds with mine. Making it a moment we can remember, a moment we could freeze in time.

You have the most incredibly beautiful crystal brown eyes that melt my heart and soul. And when caught in the gentle, bittersweet warmth of your smile it was then my heart you stole.

What lies beyond those beautiful eyes is a mystery that needs to be broken. And in the depth of night it is where I'll find the answer without a word spoken.

For when the sun descends the moonlight reveals a body of soft silky skin. A beauty so elegantly shaped it arises in me a hunger that burns within.

I want to show you an endless love and intimacy you have never felt before. And I will savor every moment for no other woman have I want more.

To have you fall asleep in my arms as I breathe the sweet fragrance of your long beautiful brown hair. Cuddled up together in the warmth of our bodies untouched by the predawn chill of the early morning air.

As I felt a cool breeze I awoke with the feeling that I had been touch by an unknown love. It wasn't until I look on my pillow that I knew you were sent from the Heavens above.

To a special friend Monica.
- Jeremy Swanson

"If only tomorrow would come"

It's been seven months since you've taken your love away. And it's been lonely without you and I think of you night and day.

I know living with me was sometimes hard and I'm sorry I didn't give all I could to you. But when I said I love you those words will always stay until the end of time and it will stand true.

For I loved you more than words and time could ever have shown. I am your soul mate and friend I hope you leave this world knowing.

Since you broke my heart I never wanted to look back nor think about. But it would mean giving up on our dreams and I can't do that when my heart is still left in doubt.

To know what forever really means I know we could be the one. And our hearts could love again if only tomorrow would come.

- Jeremy Swanson

"Given the chance I'll steal you heart"

Mary Kay if put trust in my love I promise to love you the best I can. And I'll show you that being with me is the closest to Heaven you've ever been. For rules were meant to be broken and you and I will break them all. And together we will enter into a world where love conquers all. I will be your hero and be the one to kiss away all your pain. And with me you will never be lonely or feel unloved again. And with each tomorrow as you awaken in my arms you'll know you weren't mistaken. For taking the chance and handing me that heart worth breaking. And I have only one thing to say to your mother and father. That this bad boy is going to steal the heart of their "Angel" one way or another.

-JT

"Do dreams ever come true"

Mary Kay you have the face of an Angel and green eyes as beautiful as diamonds when the moon shines light upon your face. Laying underneath the sky with you that night will be a memory that will never be lost and hard to replace. The feel of your skin held against mine steals my breath and takes me to another place in time. Where dreams become reality putting me alone without you again still wishing that you were mine. I wish I could help you live all those dreams you hold deep in your heart everyday. How I wish that I could be there holding you in my arms while you sleep as the darkness ends yet another day. Someday I'll show you that you don't have to close your eyes to dream because your dreams have always been right here with me. Now I lay awake thinking of you and thinking if only I could touch you if only you'd set your heart free.

- Jeremy Swanson

My beautiful friend: Mary Kay

"When the sun goes down"

I've prayed for a miracle to come and change my life and find a path to a better world. Little did I know I would find it all in the eyes of a beautiful green eyes girl. I thought wow! What a friend you'd be we are like two of a kind. Someone with all your qualities I thought would be impossible to find. But as fate plays it's mystery role we found a friendship in the words we send. It may only seem a short time, but "God" I would miss you if it ever had to end. I would miss the happiness and the fun you've brought into my lonely days. And how you made me smile and touch my heart in so many ways. Mary Kay you have a heart that's wild and free like the heart of a wild horse that no one can tame. It is a heart like that, that a man like me would love to claim. I what to say thank you for being a beautiful friend I've found. And I want for one day to be holding you in my arms when the sun goes down, Thank you for making me happy today!

I remember when we will in my bed, and I watched you sleep.

I'm was afraid to let my feel open, but you made me heart free.

My love is the blanket covering you.

My love is the moonlight on your face.

My love hovers over you like a Angel .

When you are awake you will think you are in Heaven!

When you are with me it's pretty close! Haha!

- Jeremy Swanson (JT Swany)

"In my heart you'll always be"

I have seen a lot of beauty in the world from the very ground I walk to the star-lit skies. And I thought I'd never see anything as beautiful again until the day I looked into your eyes.

I gazed into eyes that seemed to bring me straight to your heart and soul. And I was taken back by a beauty and love I had never known.

I thought to myself could my prayers have been answer and this feeling be real. How could this woman who just walked into my life, my heart so easily steal.

As I lay here I look out my window into the night wondering if your lonely or how you are. And a loneliness settles on my heart wishing the distance between us wasn't so far.

I hope are hearts will remain together, I guess after time we'll see. But no matter what happens Mary Kay I want you to know in my heart you'll always be.

To: my best friend Mary Kay

-Jeremy Swanson

"Hoping to make love with Mary Kay"

Everyday I look at your pictures and I'm thinking about making love to you as I go to sleep. I then close my eyes and the wildest dream that I have are of me and you, I will always keep.

I hope it will happen, what a beautiful feeling it would be, I close my eyes hoping to see your face next to me.

Hold on tight baby, for I've give you my heart, soul and the best sex any day. I will bring you to my world, you will be in Heaven that special day.

You'll feel the sexual desire we will have and the passion we will felt. I have the power to make your body melt.

I whisper your name and say I love you so much and I want to be with you. I want you by my side I imagine us together, Mary Kay make it true.

When we fucked the first time it was unreal, and we will never forget it. Mary said, it's the best sex I ever had in my life.

So cum and get more!
-Jeremy Swanson & Mary Kay

October 2011

"Only a thought away"

At times it may seem that we are two worlds apart, but the
distance between us can be brought together with only a
look of an eye. For tonight if we both look into the night we
will see the same stars that light up the very same sky.

And if you whisper softly to me I will hear you call
my name through the crisp, clear night air. Like a
voice from an Angel from the Heavenly skies telling
me that I'm not alone telling me you are there.

And no matter the distance my love I want you to know
that my love for you, will never rest. And there is nothing I
wouldn't do for you, for you I'd give my very last breath.

I want you to be my someone and help me make all my
dreams come true. For all the pain and loneliness I once
carried seems to disappear when I'm with you.

So tonight when the darkness settles look out your window
and that one lonely star you will see. And let it be that
star tonight that will bring you closer here to me.

To: Andrea
New Years Eve 2002

- *Jeremy Swanson*

"Wishing I could bring back yesterday"

Yesterday we were so happy and thought nothing could ever take that away. Little did I know that it could possibly end this way.

Sadness fills my heart when I think of the day they took me away. And now I sit here wishing I could bring back yesterday.

I think of the love we made and the laughs we shared throughout our life. But now that fateful night has severed our love like a knife.

I lay awake missing the sheltering arms of you to rest me from the day. For now all I got is to watch the sun fall as the daylight fades away. Wishing I could bring back yesterday.

- Jeremy Swanson

"A smile so sweet"

I lay awake at night with the vision of your face. Wishing
I could meet you beyond this stone walled place.

To hold you in my arms and feel you next to
me. If only I could if only I was free.

The sweetness in your smile could touch a strong mans heart. For it
did mine and now the times we see each other seems so far apart.

The beauty in you goes way beyond skin deep. Because I
can see more than just a woman with a smile so sweet.

- Jeremy Swanson

" Wishing you were here "

Tonight I want to show you that dreams really do come true. For I've waited for the night to look into those eyes while I'm making love to you. Being with me you'll never have to close your eyes to experience a dream tonight. For I'll be your dreams if you'll share with me this night. So let me show you a love that's true. And I know you'll love me back before the night is through. When consumed by the fire your body creates my heart burns with a passion. And together we will create a love neither of us could ever have imagined. When the darkness enfolds and the moon shines light upon your skin I see a flawless beauty I want to forever hold. And I can't wait for daylight to come when the full sun turns your beautiful body to a vivid gold. I wish I could turn back time and relive those dreams and make them all come real. For never in my life has any other love I felt ever compared to how you feel. I would love you always and just you only. And I promise I'll never leave you with days sad or nights lonely. If I had you by my side all my pain and loneliness would disappear. Now I lay awake missing the sheltering arms of you and wishing you were here.

-Jeremy Swanson

"Connie"

I thought it would be easy like the poems I used to write before, but I was wrong. So Connie believe in me and just read this poem and follow along. You're incredibly beautiful, everything about you seems like a dream and the warmth of your smile made my heart melt. You're the most elegantly shape woman I have seen and the passion I suddenly felt. I want to do everything that is forbidden here ,I want to hold you for the first time. The taste of your gorgeous lips when we embraced, was finer than any wine anyone could find. You don't have to say a word, your body say's it for you and your curves brings out the sexual desire in me. Your body is so beautiful, and you look so pretty with those crystal eyes, I wish you were free.

I broke the rules, either way, I'll never forget you! I did treatment, 45 days in Vinland Center was nice. I write this poem for you. Take care.

- Jeremy Swanson

"Go with your heart"

There are many ways to be yourself, but for me I have chosen to be wild and free. And because of that I have had the chance to view the world for all there is to see. I live for all that life can offer, seeking out and challenging all that's forbidden. By over stepping my bounds, breaking the rules and enjoying the life I'm liven. To feel it all you must be willing to take some risks and let your heart free and your feeling show. For if you don't take the chance, the full extent of your wildest dreams you'll never know. I've had to face life's sorrow, but I have also experienced some of the most wonderful dreams it has to hold. And the riches we can feel from all the love and happiness is worth much more than all the mountains of emeralds and gold. There is a wild and yet tame side of me that you have heard of, but never seen. And if you dare to share I with me you will see that I am the King and baby you will be my Queen. For I can make you feel like you can reach up and touch the stars above. But are you willing to take the chance when a night with me could possibly leave you falling in love. To you I would hand my heart, it's a chance I would be willing to take anytime. And though everyday hearts are broken, your I couldn't possibly break for you'd always be mine. We have all been dealt some good hands, and even the bad ones we've learned to win and put those losing cards on the shelf. So don't ever let anyone deal your cards, if you want a winning hand go with your heart and deal them yourself.

-Jeremy Swanson

"A New Beginning"

I lay awake and think of the days gone by and the night wasted all alone. I should've changed my ways, but the drinking life all I've known. So now I must face these walls as the love of my life disappears. And when I get all I'll have the memories of those wonderful years. She stayed with me and fought the odds, but now she's walked away. She didn't want to wake up every morning with hope in her heart that it would be a different day. When she looked at me I could see in her eyes the hurt and despair. For every morning at six a.m. already in front of me the whiskey was there. I felt sorry and ashamed I had start so soon. But if I had the d.t's would have killed me by noon. So I finish my drink and kissed her goodbye as I walked out the door. Knowing damn well she couldn't take it no more. I had hurt in my heart and anger all over inside. Anger at myself for needing a bottle to hide. I came home at night tired and sore from working and drinking all day. The wife wanted to talk the kids wanted to play. But for me it was that drink first I had wanted so bad. Not realizing I was taking for granted all the things that I had. Now year after year I sit here and no longer have the happiness and love that once filled my heart and home. I want my freedom, but I don't want to leave here and have to fee so all alone. I've been fighting with my life way to long it's times a new life I start living. And when I leave here I will pray to God that he help me find a new beginning.

- Jeremy Swanson

"Behind the walls"

I look out at the city lights as they flicker on. For
a time of sadness for another day is gone.

A day that can never be relived only told. A day
that could have been as precious as gold.

My cellmates have now become my life while I am here.
Reality only comes back when I look in the mirror.

I don't know how long I must live in this six-by-eight
cell. Until I am released from this living hell.

Today the sun is out, but the warmth I cannot feel. The
thought of one day being free doesn't seem real.

But as the days pass I'm closer to being free. The new
man that walks out I hope that you can see.

-Jeremy Swanson

"Hold me while I'm here"

I've been strong in heart and fought the odds in every way, but only one has brought me close to fate. When I walked out that door the last time I knew when I can back it would be too late. But I will never give up my dreams until the day I take my very last breath. Even when the day comes and they cover me with dirt my love for you will never rest.

For years I've walked the streets with pride and no fear of those around. But to ever feel again a wholeness and happiness I have never found. For inside I still live with a pain that never seems to go away. Because of my pride I lost the woman I loved when I chose to fight that summer day. So now I struggle with my life because of the choice I made and live with years of regret. It's hard to wake up and face every morning when my heart and the world won't let me forget. Many times I have stared into the star-lit sky and wished I was there. But until I had finished what I started I couldn't go anywhere. Night after night I would sit and deal the cards of life and each time pulled only the deuce. So again I would grab the bottle and needle and hit the streets to let my feelings loose. There came a night people believe I should have met my fate. But I pushed myself from the floor filled with anger and a look of hate. Taking another hit I stood my ground wiping the blood from my eyes. For I had no fear I would die until I told the ones I love my last goodbyes. When I awoke I smile in spite of all the pain for I had beat the odds again. And suddenly I turned my head and looked into the eyes of an Angel who brought me back to life when she walked in. If only she knew how much life she brought back to me and how her presence brightens cloudy skies. For she need not say a word for I feel what she expresses through her heart and trough her eyes. When she left I knew no matter how many times I had the wish to die and leave my past behind. I could not put her through that again for her a better way of life I would find. I wish I could tell her thank you for leaving me with a will to live and for placing a little happiness in my heart that day. I wish I could do the same for her for all those times she has done it for me, I know I will find a way. I will always hold the hand of death and Gods Angels are always near. Part of me is already so don't wait to hold me while I'm here.

-*Jeremy Swanson*

I has a plate in my head now, because I was in the refrigerator to get a beer, and someone hit me with a baseball ball. I got up from the floor and turned around and he hit me again in my head and I couldn't see. He put me in the back of his pickup and went to my house. My friend found me in the grass and called the emergency. I was in the hospital in St. Paul for 6 months, I couldn't talk, read, or write. I wrote this poem after 4 months I was there. I didn't push charges on Puska, I was mad I figured I will take care of it. I grew up after a few months and said, heck with it!

-*Jeremy Swanson*

"Looking from the inside out"

I said I'd never come back I was tired of doing all this time. I'll get out quit drinking and then my life will be just fine.

But again I couldn't take all the hurt and loneliness that came my way. So I hid from reality by keeping high everyday.

In the morning before work I drank my breakfast consisting of whiskey and beer. It was enough to keep away the shakes, d.t's and paranoid fear.

In my cooler was never a lunch only a bottle that kept me hidden. From all the shit and lonely life that I was liven.

For on the outside I looked happy and always carried a smile. But on the inside I wished I could put away the bottle and be myself for awhile.

But it was easier to get high and turn and walk away. Then face all the shit in my life everyday.

I've done eight years in and out since the summer of 1985. And I still continue to drink and with it the consequences of doing time.

As I sit here I say to myself when will all this end this can't be what my life is all about. God help me, I'm tired of always looking from the inside out.

- Jeremy Swanson

"Lord take me away"

It's scary to think that one day I may spend the rest of
my life locked behind a metal door. And I wonder when
the day will come when I just can't take it no more.

Everyday that passes take a little of my heart and soul away each
day. I don't want to leave here, but it hurts to much to say.

I'd like to see my family smile just once before I leave. Because
I know in their hearts, in me they no longer believe.

I can't understand why I continue to choose a life of drugs and
booze. When in this game of chance I will always continue to lose.

There's another world inside of me that you may
never see. For beyond the happiness and laughter
the pain and loneliness is slowly killing me.

Part of me is already gone and death is always near. And
tomorrow may be to late so hold me while I'm here.

And when the day finally comes and I can never again
feel the sun on my face. I'll pray that the Lord take me
far away to a better and more beautiful place.

- Jeremy Swanson

"Work farm"
(N.E.R.C.C.)

They took me from society and placed me at the farm.
They want me off their streets so I cause no future harm.

They place me on a job I work from 8 to 4.
I made a dollar a day and not a penny more.

They try to keep us busy and happy as can be.
By giving us our satellite and recreation to.

But we are not happy because of where we are.
It's not a bad place but home is better off by far.

- Jeremy Swanson

"Out of the darkness"

Each night I close my eyes to a darkness that still lies deep within my heart. For it was not long ago I knelt in prayer for a happy life and a new start. These places have brought me times of sadness and loneliness and love from my heart they tried to steal. And they had, for over the years I lost the will to love and begin confusing what is real. And when you came into my life I was still afraid to feel and let my new life begin. I thought it easier not to love then go through the hurt of losing someone again. But being with you brought me the happiness I so long deserved, but now wasn't sure I wanted to feel. For I remember the pain and the hurt that I felt before that left me scars and wounds that took forever to heal. But I know tonight will be different and when I close my eyes the darkness will no longer be there. Instead there will be thoughts of you and good times we will continue to share. I am no longer afraid to love or let myself feel what is real and true. And I can once again be myself and release the man I am inside all because of you. And when you see me again I will look and feel alive. And when our bodies come together it will be like making love for the first time. So until then hold me in your thoughts and your love keep sending. And when you see and feel me again you will wish you could keep the day from ending.

-Jeremy Swanson

"Same star different wish"

So many nights I sat at the window with a tear in my eye looking
for that one lonely stare and a wish I held deep in my heart.
Filled with so much hurt and shame that the wish had been for
the world and me to fatally part. I had hurt the one I love and for
me it was a failure I could never out live. For in my heart was the
happiness and understanding and love I so much wanted to give.
But I could no longer show the love and understanding no matter
how much I tried. For while over the years that I drank to kill the
pain and shame my will to live had also died. The shame I tried to
drink away only came back and with it a voice that said, "You're
a failure you'd be better off dead. What my family didn't know
was the pain I could no longer face. And the daily to the Lord to
take me home to Heaven because somehow here I had lost my
place. Over the last nine months I let my pain, hurt and shame
out and face each day. There were days I got down on my knees
crying and to the lord I did pray. That he help me become the
man I've hidden for so many years. And to give me the heart and
the courage to face my worse of fears. Even though today I'm in
prison I can still smile inspire of all that I have lost along the way.
Because the Lord gave me another chance at life and to live it to
the fullest everyday. Just tonight while looking out the window my
mind suddenly went amiss. For there was that same lonely star I
had always seen only tonight I hold in my heart a different wish.

- Jeremy Swanson

"The magic liquid"

It's like magic though to people it seems. But in the
end it brings nothing, but shattered dreams.

It eventually gets us no matter who we are. And it
has the power to leave our bodies a scar.

But the feeling was so nice I decided to follow the way.
Of that magic liquid who keeps me high everyday.

I drank in the morning, I drank through the night. At time
it made me happy and at times it made me fight.

And in the end it brought sorrow and to my eyes
a tear. But yet it was still magic for it made all
the important things in my life disappear.

-Jeremy Swanson

"Too drunk to walk"

I knew I had a few too many beers, but I got in my car, I was pretty drunk, but it wasn't all that far.

So on I went just to make it home. How dumb was I to think I'd be on the road all alone.

For there he was and on went the flashing lights. I knew then I wouldn't make it home that night.

I got arrested and now I sit in the county jail. And to think from the bar to my house was only a fifty-foot trail.

- Jeremy Swanson

"A letter for inside the walls"

A lay here and I wonder will I ever meet the girl I know as Bree. Or will she only become a memory when I'm finally released and free.

If I could make a wish it would be to have you here cuddled to my side. Drifting off together in love like the oceans tide.

To take your kisses so soft and sweet. Then give you mine from your head to your feet.

If you will give me only a moment of your time. I'll guarantee you'll want to be mine.

And if you ever need me I'll be there. And the love we made we'll continue to share.

So when you close your eyes tonight think of me. And when I close mine I'll think of you Bree.

-Jeremy Swanson

"I hope we meet again"

I know the length we had to know each other wasn't
a lot of time. But I hope when you leave there you'll
keep me in your heart as you will be in mine.

For you weren't just a name and a face, but became a friend. For
you made my days complete and bring smiles in the letter you send.

I wish I could of met you and maybe shared a kiss.
For it is not the mail, but it is you that I will miss.

I hope life brings you the love and happiness that you
deserve and more. And how I wish that I could be
the man outside that meets you at the door.

For when you leave I will once again feel the emptiness
that once filled my heart and soul. But you will always
be on my mind and I'll think of you where ever I go.

-Jeremy Swanson

"Through the glass"

I won't forget the times the times she brought the laundry as I watched that sweet little ass. Not knowing she was thinking who's that old man behind the glass.

I tried to look my best, I chanced my clothes, I even combed my hair. I would of stood there waiting for hours but I'm old and needed a chair.

I maybe old but I'm as sweet as cherry pie. And now since Viagra sex is worth a try.

So when you come again and see that man at least give him a smile. Cause seeing it from your sweet lips will make the memory last awhile.

(I write this poem when I was in jail about 1988)

-Jeremy Swanson

"The road alone"

The months I spent in prison slowly took away the happiness and brought pain and sorrow to what was once a good life. And now the old memories we made together are replace with new and happier ones for you, but for me they are replaced with unpleasant memories of losing my wife. And everyday I have the unpleasant task of accepting the naked truth that our past is behind us and tomorrow has yet to come along. I believe we would be together forever, but once again you have proved me wrong.

Before I came here I had a wife and a couple of friends who said their love had no bounds. But when I really needed someone the most their so-called love was nowhere to be found. Sure at one time our love was grand and I felt like a King wearing a crown. But today it's that same love that makes me feel so down.

I've learned to depend on God and myself when my loved ones were nowhere to be found. And though the pain is still real I've moved on and can live sound. So when you read these words I hope they don't find you sad. I only wrote them to bring closure to the past and say goodbye to those I love who let their love go bad.

- Jeremy Swanson

"Heart of stone"

I try to let go and find some peace from all the memories of the love we closely shared. But it's hard to forget the night we laid in bed and told each other how much we cared.

We lift each other up when we were down and at times we need simply say. I love you and always will and it brought us through the day.

The dreams I've kept in my heart will always stay until the end of time. And I still awake every morning and pray again you'll be mine.

For I would've took emeralds from mountains, star form the sky and given my love both night and day. So please don't expect me to pretend I don't love you and just walk away.

I do try to let all the hurt inside me die and forget the love I've know. But as much as I try I can't for God never gave me no heart of stone.

-Jeremy Swanson

"Heavens gate"

I had a dream I passed away and stood before the gate.
In that instant I knew I had finally met my fate.

When God came to me I asked how can this be. He said
"you had your chance at life, but gave it back to me,"

I said I don't understand everything in my life had
seemed okay, "Maybe so, but your body died from
drinking and now it is here you must stay."

So I walked to the edge of Heaven and as I look over, my family
I could see. They had sadness in their hearts all because of me.

But I wouldn't quit drinking and down that lonely road I
continued to travel. And now here I was looking down
from above as they covered me with gravel.

I miss you and when your memory will remain for I will
carve your name deep into Heavens Golden Stair.

- Jeremy Swanson

"Love me when I'm gone"

One day when my poems have stopped and my words
are no longer there to see. My tired eyes will have
closed and a gravestone will tower over me.

And under my name it will say "He will bring with him a
love that he would never let go and his happiness it cost".
For he chose to live the years without any love for the
little piece of Heaven that God had given him he lost.

He will have died alone, but it was better to have loved
and lost than never to loved at all. For the gift of love
was the greatest treasure God could give any or all.

I don't want the people to mourn or the children to cry
for I have found rest from the pain. So please let them
know that I had tried and save me from the shame.

I once wrote a poem about God painting you now
he has painter a city for me. Where I can go live in
happiness and my soul will finally be free.

I'm sorry for leaving you heart-broken and taking away
all the dreams we've held so long. I will pray that one
day you'll forgive me and love me when I'm gone.

-Jeremy Swanson

"Holding On"

I sit at the window and watch the sun disappear wondering if you think of me as I think of you. And I can feel something inside and I ask myself is my heart really being true.

At times I try to understand why this had to happen and it isn't easy being strong. And the days and nights get lonely when I can't forget you're gone.

Hearts are broken everyday, but when do we stop chasing our dreams and finally let go. Is it what might have been that our hearts keep fighting to know.

Before I let you say goodbye think of me tonight and remember the nights and love we did share. And whenever you're lonely and the darkness falls on your heart think of me and I'll be there.

There's nights I lay and wonder could it all have continued to last. And I have no doubt that it's never to late to wipe the dust from our past.

- Jeremy Swanson

"*Rule the world of love together*"

You say you're a lot to handle, well baby I'm here to prove you wrong. And I've been waiting for you way to long. Tonight I want to bring you to another world you've never been before. Where the desire and ecstasy is so great it will leave you wanting more. I want you to surrender to my love for just one day. So I can tell you all the things I've always wanted to say. All it takes is to look into those beautiful blue and I love everything I see. And tonight I want to be with you and I hope you'll be with me. The way the moonlight shines, the smooth silky skin of your body gleams. It conceals every curves of your body and makes you more beautiful than any dreams. The way you move over me like sunshine, warms everything you touch. Feeling your smooth sensual heat of your body is tantalizing me way too much. I want to hold you in my arms and kiss you long and hard as I savor every moment as our bodies enfold together. Stephanie it will be you and I that will remember that wild night we ruled the world of love together.

-Jeremy Swanson

"It's time to say goodbye"

These past years of life have been lonely and full of tears
and tired eyes that have seen far to much pain for one
man to bear. There will soon come a day when these tired
eyes go dry and I can no longer shed a tear or care.

I've been in the darkness looking and praying for the answer, but
my life keeps slipping farther each day. So I must take the fall and
hope the Angels are there so I can grab their wings and fly away.

If God lets me enter the golden gates my soul will
finally be free. And I promise not to forget you,
please do the same and not forget me.

Yesterday I walked through Heavens garden and ran my
hand over a blooming rose and it's silk petals felt as soft and
beautiful as your face. I thought of you then and how I wish
you were here, how I wish you could see this beautiful place.

When at night if you ever think of me just look into the star-
lit sky for I won't be far. Because I'll always be looking down
on you and if you wish I'll send my love in a shooting star.

And if you could whisper you love me just one more
time I will here it echo across the sky. And oh! how
I'll have wished I would of lived instead of died,

Live all you can and live all those
dreams you hold deep in your heart.
-*Jeremy Swanson*

"I've been forgotten"

You said, "I hope you never stop loving me" and I never did, but
you stopped loving me that July day. You took a big piece of my
heart that took many years and tears to wash those memories away.

I'm glad I didn't know the way it all would end until
we were through. Even though I could of missed all
the pain I then would of missed loving you.

I know one day I'll be happy and free and not have to look
out my cell at night to try and see the stars. Instead I will be
on the deck of my house that could've both been ours.

I wish I could explain some things to you, but the
words right now I cannot find. I've moved on long ago,
but I will always love you until the end of time.

Life has been patiently waiting for me and now I must
chase my dreams before I die. I don't know if I'll ever
see you again so it's time to say a real goodbye.

- Jeremy Swanson

"Losing it all"

I remember the fourth of July day I was slammed to the ground shackled and cuffed. As I rode to the jail I wondered when will I ever have enough. As I sat and stared through the bars of my cell a tear rolled down my face. Because I knew I'd drink again and prison or death was the next phase. My heart was broken because I knew it wouldn't be long before my life would end. I'd die a failure no one to love me I hadn't even a friend. I thought no one loved me and after awhile even that seemed okay. I lived with hate and destroyed anything that got in my way. At one time I had all the things a young man could ever hold. Now here I was in prison locked away from it all as I watched my life unfold. As I lay in my cell I thought of all those dreams I'd leave behind. And my kids I love so much hung heavily on my mind. I can't give up I said up myself as I got down on my knees. And in the darkness of that cell I prayed to God to hear my pleas. That was a year ago and now I will soon be released and my new life will start. Because of the love for my kids and refusing to give up on my dreams that night I gave God my heart. At that moment I was finally set free and though in prison I still dwell. I am happy for I've change my life and saved myself from years of hell.

- Jeremy Swanson

"Never say goodbye"

You can't say goodbye to love you can only put it on hold. For
when you love someone like we did it lasts until were old.

Feeling such a closeness when we held each other tight.

Can never be taken away for in our hearts we stored every night.

I remember when we would fight and neither of
us would give in. We both would of liked to say
sorry, but then neither of us would win.

I used to watch you walking around the house and laying
there in your sleep. And I said to myself and the Lord
"This is the woman I'll always love and try to keep.

The laughs and the smiles I shared with you are planted
deep within my heart. I can think back and still feel
those times even though were miles apart.

Loving someone is great and it keeps you feeling free.
But I felt it was more than that with you and me.

So when your lonely Sheila don't ever feel sad or
alone just remember what I've told, That we never
said goodbye we just put or love on hold.

-Jeremy Swanson

"The time to say goodbye"

Your smiles and laughter I'll always remember and
goodbye is hard to say. And I wonder without
such a friend if I'll make it through the day.

I thank God for giving me such a friend who kept
my heart alive and stronger. It was fun and though
life goes on I wish it would have lasted longer.

You are truly an Angel one that deserved the best in life. And
there's one lucky man that will soon have you to gall his wife.

I wish you the love and happiness that anyone could ever receive.
And I won't ever forget you, please do the same and not forget me.

- Jeremy Swanson

"I'm no Angel at all"

I was sent from Heaven to make sure you get all the love and special attention you deserve. And being with me is the closest to Heaven you'll ever be while still here on Earth.

I'll chase away the ghosts out from under your bed and take away all the fear. While I whisper intimate fantasies softly in your ear.

You are a true temptation and the way you make me feel when I touch your beautiful silky skin. Makes me want to shed my wings and bring out the devil I've held within.

Tonight I want to be your everything and you to be mine. For I've looked long for such a truly rare and precious find.

I will show you a love that will make you feel like you can reach up and touch all the stars in the sky. I will always be here for you and my promise to you will never die.

I can make the Heavenly rains fall and the sun to shine bright everyday. And it will be the rains from Heaven that will wash all your doubts away.

I said I was sent from heaven, but a wild night out with me will prove I'm no Angel at all. So watch your step sweetheart because with me love is where you just might fall.

-Jeremy Swanson

"Thanksgiving"

Thanksgiving is a time of peace and togetherness in all years through. A time to chow their food and guzzle all their brew.

The day finally ends when your stuffed and juiced as hell. Knowing you sacrificed a turkey makes you feel like hell.

-Jeremy Swanson

"Always in our hearts"
In loving memory of (Skipper) Kainz

The talks, the laughter, the times we just spent in silence, are missed so dearly without you here. For together we shared our hopes, our dreams and talked of our fear. The days are filled with emptiness since the day our lives became severed. It seems like until the end, we looked at life like it would last forever. But on Nov. 14th, God took home another special life that touched many a hearts and has left us with sadness and anger for how quickly life can part. You'll always be remember for the love and the smile you shared with us everyday. And even though you're gone, the great memories you left can never be taken away.

We love and miss you dearly, "Skipper"! Jeremy
and Barney Swanson and their children. Jerry
Dean, Nancy and Cubby and their families.

-Jeremy Swanson

"In memory Leonore (Skipper) Kainz"

Another year has passed and another sun has set, as we look
back four years on a time and a woman we will never forget.
We lost a special mother and grandmother who was true in our
hearts forever with the beautiful memories you've left behind.

In good times and in bad you always seemed to find the
strength and the courage to carry on. We try to do the same,
but at times it isn't easy when we can't forget you've gone.

But we know you are in a beautiful place where you
can now feel a peace within. And we only said goodbye
for now, for one day we will be together again.

We all love and miss you very much and you'll always be in our
hearts forever. May God bless you with all that Heaven can offer.

-Jeremy Swanson

"*A mothers love*"
"In memory of Leonore (Skipper) Kainz"

If you were here today I would tell you just how much I truly care. For giving me the love and support I needed in life and always being there. You know that I love you and you love me, but even now I wish we had said it more. Because we can never count on tomorrow for we never know what it has in store. While you were here you showed me just how precious life can be. And how you faced life's challenge and lightened the way for me. You showed me that when times get tough love can conquer all. And you were there to take my hand whenever I took that fall. Most of all you showed me how strong a mothers love can be when facing the worst. And even in those times you needed the love the most you made sure we had it first. Through it all you were there for me when I needed that special friend. And you showed that incredible courage, love and heart you had right up until the end.

A thought in memory:

Remember those times of joy and even the times of sorrow for today they may not seem like much. But tomorrow they could be the only memories we have when the people we love are no longer there to touch.

-*Jeremy Swanson*

"In memory of Nancy Kainz Karsten"

Even though we all know the ones we love can leave this world at anytime. It's still makes it really hard to face the loneliness, emptiness and pain we all feel every time.

But I know Nancy can smile and is happy now because I myself dream of Heaven and what Heaven would be like when God ever asks for you or me. And to realize how precious she was on earth with the caring for God creatures and people is plain to see.

She was always happy with what she had and the animals she could teach. Nothing ever passed her by, for her everything to make her happy was always within reach.

Now she can walk through Heavens Garden and run her hands over the blooming roses and its silk petals that are as soft and beautiful as her face. And she will tell you then not to cry, she'll look around and watch the doves fly and wish we all could see that beautiful place.

A thought in memory: Every minute that we spend today doesn't seem like much. But tomorrow people we love can no longer be there to touch. Remember when the lord takes us away it's to always to a better and more beautiful place, so it's okay to cry, because happiness is with her now, so smile too!

-Jeremy Swanson